DELIVERANCE BOOKS

Blood of Jesus

Its Benefits and How to Use it Effectively

In the name of the Father, and of the Son, and of the Holy Spirit

The streaming wounds of Jesus are the sure guarantees for answered prayer.

— CHARLES SPURGEON

Contents

Preface

This book is a deliverance manual geared towards those who are into self-deliverance and deliverance for others. It's also intended to help those who want to grow spiritually.

It gives you a basic understanding of the meaning and importance of the Blood of Jesus, its power, and how to use it effectively.

Precious Blood

*I*n the beginning, God said, "Let there be light and there was light." The light came from God, and the light itself is God. The Spirit of God is light, and the light itself is life. That same life is blood; the blood of Jesus Christ, the blood of the Almighty God. For the Father, the Son, and the Spirit are one.

Everything that God created was done with the Word of God. The Word was with God, and the Word was God. Jesus is the Word of God.

And he was clothed with a vesture dipped in blood: and his name is called The Word of God. And the armies which were in heaven followed him upon white horses, clothed in fine linen, white and clean. Rev 19:13-14 (KJV)

On the cross of Calvary, God gave his blood for the salvation of humanity. He gave all he had, his own life so that he could save us. God does not joke with the blood of Jesus. In all that you do, do not neglect the blood of Jesus, for there is no other part to victory. **By his blood, you overcome and conquer all**.

And one of the elders answered, saying unto me, What are these which are arrayed in white robes? And whence came they? And I said unto him, Sir, thou knowest. And he said to me, These are they which came out of great tribulation, and have washed their robes, and made them white in the blood of the Lamb. Rev 7:13-14 (KJV)

Benefits

Redemption

If we are to be reconciled with God, we have to be redeemed. If we are not redeemed, we can't have a relationship and fellowship with God. When Adam disobeyed God, sin entered humanity, which resulted in spiritual death. Jesus came so we would get eternal redemption. By his blood, we are redeemed and reconciled with God.

In whom we have redemption through his blood, the forgiveness of sins, according to the riches of his grace. Eph 1:7 (KJV)

Atonement of Sin

The blood of Jesus atones for all sins. It doesn't matter what sin we have committed. It atones for ancestral sins, community sins, family sins, and individual sins.

When you pray that the Lord should wash away your sins, also pray that he should also wash away inherited sin in your life, so that your spiritual garment will be completely clean.

And he is the propitiation for our sins: and not for ours only, but also for the sins of the whole world. 1 Jn 2:2 (KJV)

Tracy had problems in her marriage. This was her third marriage heading for a divorce. She was a good person, but for some reason, all her relationships always ended up in disaster. She wanted her third marriage to survive. She was willing to fight for it.

Tracy approached a man of God, a prophet who prayed for her. After praying, the man of God told her that the reason she was having problems in her marriage was because of a grievous sin in her life. Evil spirits used that sin as a point of contact and legal ground to cause problems in her marriage.

She told the prophet that though she wasn't the most perfect person; she was a good person. The prophet then went on to tell her that she was paying the price for the sins committed by her ancestors, notably her grandfather.

He prayed for her, and she also prayed and asked Jesus to forgive her sins and also any inherited sin in her life. Jesus forgave her, washed away her sins with his blood, and she was delivered from the evil spirits troubling her marriage.

Healing

The blood of Jesus heals. The same way the blood of Jesus washes away sins, it can also heal us from our sickness and infirmities.

But he was wounded for our transgressions, he was bruised for our iniquities: the chastisement of our peace was upon him; and with his stripes, we are healed. Is 53:5 (KJV)

Pray that the Lord should use his blood to wash away every sickness in your body, both the physical and spiritual body so that your healing may be complete.

John was suffering from a mental problem. He always had severe headaches and found it difficult concentrating. He has been going through this problem for many years. John remembered God one night and decided to ask God for healing.

That night, he fell into a trance. In the trance, he heard a voice which told him to "wash his head with the Blood of Jesus". John woke up and did exactly as instructed. He got a bowl, prayed on it, and asked God to change it into the blood of Jesus. He took the bowl of water and washed his head. John was immediately healed.

Anna was kidnapped by a group of men who wanted to use her for rituals. She was tied up, knocked unconscious, thrown in a van, and driven to an unknown destination. When she woke up, she found herself in a small room with other girls. She immediately started to plead the blood of Jesus upon her life.

Moments later, she heard a commotion coming from outside the room. The men were arguing amongst themselves. One man came into the room, dragged her out into a waiting car, blindfolded her and drove away.

After driving for a while, the car stopped. She was kicked out of the car and dumped on the side of the road. The blood of Jesus saved Anna that day. It brought confusion in the midst of the kidnappers.

Deliverance

We can use the Blood of Jesus for deliverance. Before attempting any form of deliverance, inquire from God for approval. Most people go into deliverance without God's approval and end of getting seriously attacked, making the issue worse.

The blood of Jesus will pull down strongholds, destroy idols, cast out evil spirits and destroy abominations. **It's the one solution to all spiritual problems**.

Nullifying Evil Food

We are fed with evil food in the dream to keep us spiritually weak. Not all food eaten in the dream is evil. These evil foods are sometimes masked as food we eat every day. Evil food eaten in the dream is meant to cause sickness and terrible afflictions in our life.

When you notice that you have eaten in the dream, use the Blood of Jesus to cancel it immediately after you wake up so that it becomes ineffective immediately.

Restoration of Spiritual Powers (Charismatic gifts of the Holy Spirit)

Our spiritual powers are special abilities handed down to us by the holy spirit so that we can use it for the purpose of building up the body of Christ. Each of us has a spiritual gift(s). The holy spirit distributes each gift as he sees fit. You can use the blood of Jesus to restore your spiritual gift by washing the head with the Blood of Jesus.

A pastor had a dream in which he saw his hair shrinking and a part of his head decaying. This dream meant that his spiritual powers were not functioning properly. The Pastor washed his head with the blood of Jesus to restore his spiritual powers.

Sanctification after Defilement

We can be defiled when we touch or enter places that are unholy. It's important to constantly purify yourself every day because we are continuously moving about during the day. It could be at our place of work or even places where you shop.

You can become defiled if you come in contact with or touch someone who is already defiled. You can become defiled when you enter a place buried with charms or evil objects. There are numerous ways one can become defiled, and that's why it's important that you constantly cleanse yourself with the Blood of Jesus.

Sara rented a house in a new city. She didn't know that the previous occupant of the house was a witchcraft practitioner. The previous occupant had defiled the place so much that it became an abode of evil spirits, and the whole house was covered in spiritual darkness.

Throughout the time Sara lived in that house, she did not make any progress. It was from one problem to the other. It wasn't until she left the house that things took a turn for the better. Sara should have prayed and purified the house with the Blood of Jesus before moving in.

Consecration

Quick Method

If you are in a hurry or don't have the necessary materials needed, you can use this simple method to make the blood of Jesus.

Get a bottle, a bowl, or a cup of water.

Thank God for his goodness and abundant mercy. Pray to God to send down the power of the holy spirit upon the water. Raise the water towards God's throne and ask him to change the water into the blood of Jesus.

Advanced Method

This method can be utilized for spiritual work or worship service.

Pray Psalm 24 (3) three times on the water.

Thank God for his abundant goodness. Ask for God's mercy to descend on the water. Pray for the power of the holy spirit.

Raise the bowl or cup to heaven. Give thanks to God for the blood of Jesus, the blood of power and victory that conquers all.

Pray and ask God to change this water into the blood of Jesus, the blood of the new and everlasting covenant that was shed for the salvation of humanity.

Efficacy

*T*here is great power in the blood of Jesus. **Do not neglect it.**

Then Jesus said unto them, Verily, verily, I say unto you, Except ye eat the flesh of the Son of man, and drink his blood, ye have no life in you. Whoso eateth my flesh, and drinketh my blood, hath eternal life; and I will raise him up at the last day. Jn 6:53-54 (KJV)

Use the blood of Jesus to destroy the forces of darkness

Use the blood of Jesus to destroy the strongholds of darkness

Bath with the blood of Jesus and dispel the surrounding darkness. Be consistent and the darkness will move away from you.

The Blood of Jesus Christ is a consuming fire to evil spirits and the forces of darkness. Use it to obtain victory.

Enter a place of darkness and be protected by the blood of Jesus.

Wash your feet with the blood of Jesus and neutralize charms and poisons.

The blood of Jesus will wash away your sins and make you holy. Drink it.

The blood of Jesus is victory. Perfect your victory daily by making use of the blood of Jesus daily.

Sprinkle the blood of Jesus in your home and in your environment. Sanctify, sanctify, sanctify. Dispel the darkness.

Bath with it for good health and prosperity.

Wash your hands with the blood of Jesus to restore fortune and heavenly destiny.

Worksheet

*I*n your own terms, explain the meaning of the Blood of Jesus. In what way is the blood of Jesus connected with creation?

I

Why did Jesus give his blood on the cross of Calvary?

II

*N*ame five benefits of the blood of Jesus? How does each of these benefits affect your life

III

*L*ocate five passages in the Bible connected with the blood of Jesus.

III

*I*n your own terms, explain each passage and how they can help you obtain deliverance or grow spiritually.

IV

Y ou desire to grow spiritually, how will you utilize the blood of Jesus?

Note

Recommended Reading

- Revelation 12:11

- Ephesians 2:12-13

- Ephesians 1:7

- 1 Peter 1:18-19

- Revelation 1:5

Made in the USA
Middletown, DE
06 September 2023

38125459R00018